CW00369524

ISBN 978-1-333-79546-7
PIBN 10549250

AUTHOR:

STEUART, ARCHIBALD

TITLE:

SCOTTISH INFLUENCE

PLACE:

GLASGOW

DATE:

3

COLUMBIA UNIVERSITY LIBRARIES
PRESERVATION DEPARTMENT

BIBLIOGRAPHIC MICROFORM TARGET

Original Material as Filmed - Existing Bibliographic Record

Steuart, Archibald Francis.
Scottish influences in Russian history, from the end of the 16th century to the beginning of the 19th century: an essay... Glasgow, Maclehose, 1913.
xviii, 141 p. plates, fold. table. 20 cm.

Restrictions on Use:

TECHNICAL MICROFORM DATA

FILM SIZE: 35mm REDUCTION RATIO: 11x
IMAGE PLACEMENT: IA (IIA) IB IIB
DATE FILMED: 4/4/91 INITIALS F.C.
FILMED BY: RESEARCH PUBLICATIONS, INC WOODBRIDGE, CT

AIIM
rmation and Image Management
iyne Avenue, Suite 1100
pring, Maryland 20910
301/587-8202

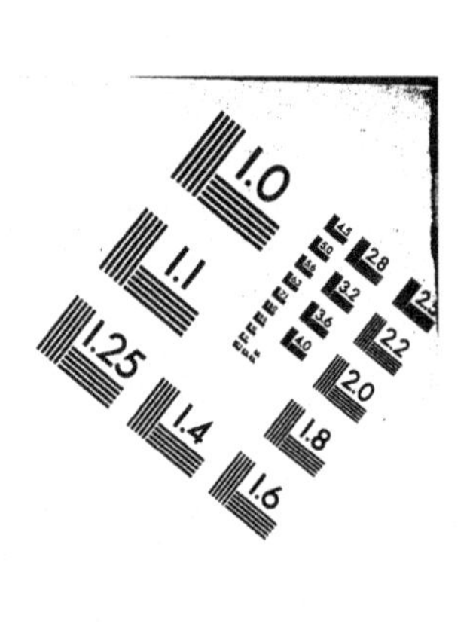

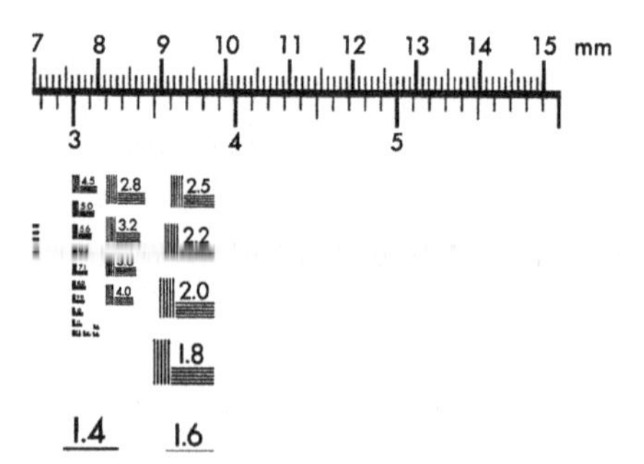

PUBLISHED BY
JAMES MACLEHOSE AND SONS, GLASGOW,
Publishers to the University.

MACMILLAN AND CO., LTD., LONDON.
New York, - - *The Macmillan Co.*
Toronto, - - - *The Macmillan Co. of Canada.*
London, - - - *Simpkin, Hamilton and Co.*
Cambridge, - - *Bowes and Bowes.*
Edinburgh, - - *Douglas and Foulis.*
Sydney, - - - *Angus and Robertson.*

MCMXIII.

TSAR ALEKSEI MICHAELOVITCH AND HIS SECOND CONSORT
NATHALIA KIRILLOVNA NARISHKINA.

Pen-and-ink Sketch by
James S. Richardson.

SCOTTISH INFLUENCES IN RUSSIAN HISTORY

FROM THE END OF THE 16TH CENTURY
TO THE BEGINNING OF THE 19TH CENTURY

An Essay

BY

A. FRANCIS STEUART

ADVOCATE

GLASGOW
JAMES MACLEHOSE AND SONS
PUBLISHERS TO THE UNIVERSITY
1913

the great empire of the Tsars, so I have endeavoured shortly to sketch the 'service' given by the Scots who enrolled themselves in the Russian employ. My book is founded, not so much on Russian, as on French and British sources, and thus the dates and the spelling of names may be sometimes irregular. It, however, claims the privilege of an explorer or that of a pioneer.

I have tried to indicate where authorities on my subject may be most easily found, and have therefore cited copiously only from the rarer and less known books.

Some day a Russian scholar will dig up lists (lists I long to see) of Scottish names from the depths of the archives of Russia. I hope he will come soon. Until he does, I trust that my essay may help the Scot to understand Russian history better, and the Russian to be interested in those of the Scottish nation who helped to connect his Byzantine civilisation, marred as it was and retarded by the Tartar conquest, with that of Western Europe.

I have to thank especially my friends Mr.

CONTENTS

CHAPTER V.

CHAPTER VI.

CHAPTER VII.

CHAPTER VIII.

CHAPTER IX.

ILLUSTRATIONS.

and Lithuania united, 1569. Polotsk and Livonia lost to Russia. Novgorod reduced and the inhabitants massacred, 1570. Treaties with Elizabeth, Queen of England. Foreigners enter Russian Military service. Siberia conquered, 1558-84.

Feodor (I.) Ivanovitch (1584-1598).

Rise of Boris Feodorovitch Godounoff, brother of the Tsaritsa Irina. The Peasant attached to the glebe and made a Serf. Treaties with Elizabeth. Murder of the Tsar's half-brother, Dmitri. End of the Dynasty of Rurik.

Boris Feodorovitch Godounoff (1598-1605).

Elected Tsar on his brother-in-law's death. Foreigners favoured. Appearance of the 'False Dmitri.'

The 'False Dmitri.'

Claiming to be the murdered **Dmitri Ivanovitch,** son of 'The Terrible' Tsar, entered Russia with Polish support. The Godounoff family murdered or cloistered. He was married in Moscow to the Polish Maryna Mniszek, who was crowned with him. Murder of the Tsar and massacre of the Poles in Moscow, 1606.

Vassili Ivanovitch Shuiski (1606). **Time of the Troubles.**

Elected Tsar. War with the Poles and the 'Second False Dmitri,' a Cossack brigand. Abdication of the Tsar, who enters a monastery.

1689, when Peter forced the Regent to take the veil, and assumed the complete power though allowing his brother the title of Tsar. Expeditions against Azof, 1695-1696. First journey to the West, 1697. Revolt and total destruction of the Streltsi. War with Sweden, ending in the battle of Poltava, 1709. Ingria taken by Russia in 1702. St. Petersburg founded, 1703, as a 'Window into Europe.' War with Turkey and Treaty of the Pruth, 1711. The Tsar visited Paris. Peace of Nystad, 1721, which gave Livonia, Esthonia, Carelia and part of Finland to Russia. The Tsar declared Autocrat. Trial and death of the Tsarevitch Aleksei Petrovitch, 1718. The Tsar declared Emperor, 1721. A doubtful will.

Catherine (I.) (1725-1727).

Widow of Peter I. Power of Menschikoff. Peter I.'s Westernisation continued.

Peter (II.) Alekzievitch (1727-1730).

Grandson of Peter I. Fall of Menschikoff. Rise of the Dolgoroukis. Return of the Court to Moscow. The Tsar buried there.

Anna Ivanovna (1730-1740).

Niece of Peter I. Elected under a constitution. Constitution abrogated. Fall of the Dolgoroukis. Rise of Biron, Duke of Courland. Return of the Court to St. Petersburg. War of the Polish succession and against the Turks, 1735-39.

CHIEF EVENTS IN RUSSIAN HISTORY

Alexander I.) (1801-1825).

Eldest son of Paul I. Napoleonic wars. Austerlitz, Eylau, etc. Interview at Erfurt. Wars with England, Sweden, Austria, Turkey and Persia. Napoleon invades Russia, 1812. Retreat of 'la Grande Armée.' Congress of Vienna. Reforms. Serfage lightened. Disquiet in Poland. The Tsar religious mystic.

CHAPTER I.

THE FIRST SCOT IN RUSSIA. SCOTS IN POLAND. THE ENGLISH 'SOCIETY FOR THE DISCOVERY OF UNKNOWN LANDS' COME TO RUSSIA. THE EMBASSIES OF IVAN THE TERRIBLE TO ENGLAND, AND HIS DESIRES. THE POLICY OF HIS SUCCESSORS.

I.

He would be a bold man who would state who was the first Scot who went to Russia. The statement, however, has been ventured on by Dr. J. Hamel in his book *England and Russia*,[1] and he says that 'Master David,' a Scot, Herald to the King of Denmark, was envoy from his master, King John, to the Grand Prince Vassili Ivanovitch, of Muscovy, in 1495. His name is commonly given as 'Geraldus,' the russification of his office of 'Herald,' but it seems to have been Kocken, Kocker, or perhaps Cock. He was probably sent to Russia with the Danish embassy in 1492, to induce the Grand Prince to seize Sweden and its dependency, Finland, in return for which the

[1] Translated into English by John Studdy Leigh, F.R.G.S., in 1854. It is very difficult to follow, but still remains the best book on the subject.

King of Denmark promised to assist Russia against Lithuania, and he returned thither the next year. He again returned in 1505 with a letter addressed to the Grand Prince, but found that the Prince had died in October; so he either remained, or was forced to remain until 1507, when new envoys had reached the new Grand Prince from Denmark, and returned with them. He seems to have been a man of mark and a trusty messenger, and he is mentioned in the letter of alliance sent by the new Tsar, Ivan Vassilievitch, to 'our brother John, King of Dacia (Denmark?) Sweden and Norway' dated at Moscow.

In the fifteenth and sixteenth centuries Scottish merchants spread in hordes all over Prussia and Poland[1] as traders, but few as yet seem, unless by chance, to have gone further East.

In the reign of Ivan Vassilievitch the English spirit of adventure which had formed 'The Society for the Discovery of Unknown Lands' first thought of Russia as a field for exploration.

[1] A book on 'Scots in Poland,' edited by Miss Beatrice Baskerville, is promised by the Scottish History Society.

A Russian Company was formed (it employed many people with curiously Scottish-sounding names like Logan, Gordon, Brighouse, etc.) which traded at Rose Island, Kholmogory on the White Sea, and later had an 'English house' in the Varvarka at Moscow; but the real settlement of the Scots in Russia, which was involuntary, and yet left a great mark on the history of Russia, was quite distinct from this body.

Ivan the Terrible had some definite idea that the way Russia had been cut off from the rest of Europe by the Tartar invasion and long subjugation had done harm. No Russian till his father's time (the Danish embassy) had been allowed to leave Russia, and it was only fear of internecine war that made him seek that friendship with England that is so curious in history. One of his ambassadors was wrecked on the coast of Scotland, Ossip Gregorievitch Nepeja, who with a suite of sixteen persons had been sent in 1556 as envoy to Philip and Mary in the 'Edward Bonaventure.' It was near Pitsligo Bay the wreck took place, and all the Tsar's presents were lost, with the English captain, Richard Chancellor, his son and seven Russians of the ambassador's suite. Robert Best, interpreter to the embassy, escaped with the ambassador. The unfortunate refugees left Edinburgh, whither they had had a 'Tal-matsch' (tolmach) or 'speachman' (*i.e.* interpreter) sent to them from London, on 14th February, 1557, with but a few trifles saved from their wreck, to begin their embassy so long hindered. This embassy was followed by others to Queen Elizabeth, who sent Randolph, Jenkinson, and Daniel Silvester to Russia; and by his ambassadors, Pissemski and Andrei Gregorievitch Savin, while he granted privileges to the English, the Tsar showed two curious definite desires. First, in the event of his long-suffering subjects putting an end to his reign, that he wished a safe residence in England; and, secondly, that he wished for an English wife, the Queen if possible, and afterwards (though he had just married his seventh wife, Maria Feodorovna Nagoi) the Queen's kinswoman, Lady Mary

Hastings, as his bride.[1] Queen Elizabeth, as her habit was, promised much but did little. To the Tsar's remonstrance about the 'bad conduct' of her subjects, she replied that the wrong-doers were probably Scots, who had strayed over the Russian border from Poland or Sweden, and so beyond her jurisdiction. She sent a physician, Dr. Robert Jacob, who favoured the English match; and the result was that a Russian ambassador, Feodor Andreevitch Pissemski, was sent to London. He returned with an English ambassador, Sir Jerome Bowes, who was well received, and succeeded (through the help of Jerome Horsey, an English agent) in getting exclusive privileges for the English merchants when the Tsar suddenly died, leaving the Tsardom to his son, the mild and feeble Feodor Ivanovitch, and the power in the hands of the latter's able and rather unscrupulous brother-in-law, Boris Feodorovitch Godounoff.

[1] This appears to have been suggested to the Tsar by his physician, Dr. Bomel (educated at Cambridge), whom he [illegible] cruelly put to death. The idea was again suggested by one Aegidius Crow.

He rose rapidly, and was named 'Prince Protector,' and proved himself the friend of foreign ways. Bowes, who had been maltreated on Ivan's death, was allowed to return home. Sir Jerome Horsey went back to Russia as ambassador in 1585, and wrote an admirable account of his travels; so did Giles Fletcher.[1] The English house in the Varvarka prospered exceedingly in spite of double dealing on every side and 'interloping' Englishmen. The Tsar died in 1598, and Boris Godounoff was elected to succeed him. In 1600 he sent an ambassador, Gregory Ivanovitch Mikulin, to Queen Elizabeth to cement the friendly understanding. It is interesting to find that he was visited in London by the Scottish ambassador (whose master, James VI., became King of England as James I. on Elizabeth's death, three years

[1] Captain Thomas Ogilvy, burgess of Dundee, was denounced for not appearing before the Privy Council of Scotland, 29th Dec., 1595, to answer to a charge of having intromitted with the goods of a Danzig ship, the property of the Duke of Florence. Among the cargo was a barrel of books, 'all of ane historie anent the descriptioun of the cuntreis of Polonia, Moscovia, Prussia & utheris adjacent, to the noumer of xxxix.'—*Register of the Privy Council of Scotland*, vol. v. p. 251.

later), the Earl of Bothwell. He tried to arrange another 'English match' for the new Tsarevitch, Feodor Borissovitch. On Queen Elizabeth's death James I. dispatched another mission to Russia, and obtained benefits for the merchants, but these were vitiated by the Tsar Boris's death and the Time of the Troubles. The first Romanoff Tsar did, however, find the English of use. They lent him money when he was bankrupt, and it was owing to the intercession of the ambassador of James I. and VI., John Merrick, who went to Moscow in 1614, that Gustavus Adolphus of Sweden, in 1617, gave up Novgorod, Roussa and Ladoga to Russia, while retaining the maritime conquests in the Baltic. This was a great gain to Russia, yet the English merchants did not receive privileges of sufficient value, owing to the opposition of the Russian traders. They continued, however, to have some success until the news of the execution of their King, Charles I., reached the Tsar Aleksei Michaelovitch, when that stalwart supporter of Royalty forbade them to exercise trade in his realm except at Kholmogory on the White Sea, and banished them from the rest of his dominions. He repaid his obligations to the Stuarts also by sending aid to King Charles II. during his long pauper-stricken exile in Holland.

CHAPTER II.

THE CAPTIVES. COMMENCEMENT OF THE COLONY OF THE SCOTS. THE FOREIGN FAUBOURG. VICISSITUDES OF SCOTTISH SOLDIERS.

II.

THE beginning of the Scottish colony in Russia was very different from that of the English merchants. The Scottish colony began as prisoners. To give the words of the Englishman, Sir Jerome Horsey:

'The Emperor's souldiers and army, farr greater in number, ranged farr into the Swethians country, and did much spoill and rapine;[1] brought many captives awaye to remote places in his land, Liefflanders, French, Scotts, Dutchmen and some English. The Emperower seatlinge and seatinge a great many of them in the

[1] In 1557-58 Livonia was ravaged by the Tsar's troops, composed mostly of savages, Mordvinians and Chermisses, who burned everything, 'not even sparing the child in its mother's womb.' The Livonians invoked Polish aid. After more war—in 1572 he raided Esthonia—the Tsar had to surrender Livonia to Poland, in 1582, by the Treaty of Zapolok. It was evidently about 1581 that the Scots were transported to Moscow.

cittie of Musquo, to inhabitt by themselves without the cittie; and by my mediacion and means, beinge their conversant and famillier in the Court, well knowen and respected of the best favorets and officers of that tyme, I procured libertie to buyld them a Churche, and contrubetted well therunto; gott unto them a learned preachinge minister, and devine service and metinge of the congregacion everie Saboth daye, but after their Lutheren profession, grew in shortt tyme in favour and famillier, and in good like of the Russ people, livinge civillie but in dollfull and mourninge manner for ther eyvill loss of goods, friends and contrye. At which tyme, among other nacions, there wear fower score and five pore Scotts souldiers leaft of 700 sent from Stockhollme, and three Englishmen in their company, brought amonge other captives, in most miserable manner, pittious to behold. I laboured and imploied my best indevors and creditt not only to succor them, but with my purse and paines and means gett them to be well placed at Bulran, near the Musquo; and altho' the Emperowr was much

inflamed with fury and wrath against them, torteringe and puttinge many of these Swethian souldiers to deth, most lamentabylie to behold, I procured the Emperower to be told of the difference between these Scottsmen, now his captives, and the Swethians, Pollonians and Livonians, his enymies. They wear a nacion strangers, remote, a venturous and warlicke people, readie to serve any Christian prince for maintenance and paye; as they would apear and prove, if it pleased his majestie to imploie and spare them such maintenance now owt of hart and cloths and arms, as they may shew themselves and valure against his mortall enemy the Cryme Tartor. Yt seems some use was made of this advice,[1] for shortly the best souldiers and men-at-arms of these straingers wear spared and putt apart, and captaines of each nacion apointed to govern the rest; Jeamy Lingett for the Scottish men, a villiant honest

[1] Ivan, in 1552, captured Kazan, and in 1555 sent Ivan Sheremetieff against Perekop with 13,000 men (R. Nisbet Bain's [illegible] against the Tartars in and out of Crimea was, no doubt, kept up, particularly after the burning of Moscow by the Tartars ('The Crimme') in 1571.

man. Mony, cloths, and dayelly alowance for meat and drincke, was geaven them, horss, hey and oatz; swords, peece and pistolls, wear they armed with. Pore snakes afore, loke nowe chearfully. Twelve hundred of them did better service against the Tartor then 12 thowsand Russes, with their shortte bowe and arrowes. The Crim, not knowinge then the use of peece and pistolls, stroken dead of their horses with shott they sawe not, cried:—"Awaye with those new divells that com with their thunderinge puffs;" wherat the Emperor made good sportt. Then had thei pencions and lands alowed them to live upon, marrid and matchd with the Livonian faire weomen;[1] increased into famillies, and live in favour of the prince and people. O! how glad was I that the Emperowr toke noe noatice of these fewe Englishmen taken captive emonge them! An oportune quarrel, to my liff, that was so well knowen and conversant in their court; but especiallie a fit prey for the Emperor to seize upon the English merchants

[1] He calls them elsewhere 'The Livonian ladies, the fairest weomen of the knowen world.'

goods, havinge a stocke in company for at least 100 thowsand marckes sterlinge in his country. For, but a littell before, the Kinge had sold to one Thomas Glover, a chieff agent for that company, a wiff bowren of a noble howse in Polland, Basmanovey, taken captive at Pellotcoe, for tenn thowsand Hengers ducketts in gold; and yet shorttly after, fallinge into som displeasur, robbed him of 16 thowsand pounds more in cloth, silke, wax, furrs and other merchandizes and sent him[1] and his deare wife emptie out of his land.'[2]

There were, one way or other, evidently a good many Scots in Russia during the time of Ivan the Terrible. Dr. Collins, the English Physician of Tsar Aleksei Michaelovitch, narrates an incident at the Court of the Terrible Tsar. 'Some foreigners, English and Scots, had laughed at certain things the Tsar had done during a drinking bout. The Tsar when he heard this had them stripped naked and

[1] He was banished from Russia in 1573. His marriage took place before 1567, when Queen Elizabeth complained to the Tsar of his conduct.—See Hamel, pp. 186, 191, 221.

[2] *Travels of Sir Jerome Horsey* (Hakluyt Society), pp. 182-184.

forced them to pick up, one by one, five or six bushels of peas which had been poured into his room. Then he gave them drink and sent them away.' That there were many is shown too by his statement that 'some old residents in Russia have noticed that out of two hundred, English, Scots and Dutch, who have embraced the Russian Faith, hardly one has died a natural death.'[1]

From his associates the English envoy, Giles Fletcher, also evidently knew something of Scottish customs. He says that in the Russian towns 'Every house hath a paire of staiers, that lead up into the chambers out of the yarde or streat, after the Scottish manner.'[2] Horsey adds another passage about the Scots later:[3]

'And the Pollonians and Swethians combynded and plotted how each of them might invade each others teritoris and anctient bounds; toke good opportunitie to recover all back again which the old Emperor Ivan had

[1] From the French Translation of Dr. Collins's *Present State of Russia* (Paris, 1679), pp. 9, 67.

[2] *The Russe Common Wealth*, p. 19.

[3] *Travels of Sir Jerome Horsey* (Hakluyt Society), p. 225.

gotten from them. . . . Some Swethen souldiers escaped thenc and came to the Musquo to serve the Emperor; among whom was one Gabriell Elphingsten, a valiant Scottish captaine, by the report of the letters he brought to me from Corronell Steward, that served the King of Denmarke, in comendacion of him and six other Scotts, souldiers in his company, but all verie bare of monny and furnitur. Desired me to grac place and suplie their necessities. I disburst to him and them 300 dollers; put them in apperrell, and bought them pistolls and swords; and when they wear marched wear better liked of then they Swedian souldiers that came in ther company. I gott Captaine Elphingstone the charge over them all, begenod (*sic*) of mony, horss, and allowancence for meat and drincke. Behaved themselves well for a tyme, yet could not repaye nor recompence me to this day, as by their letters apeareth.'

But one General Carmichael, a Scot, entered (apparently voluntarily) the service of the Terrible Tsar. Scottish history is altogether silent about him, though he was uncle to Sir

John Carmichael, Warden of the Border, of the Hyndford family. He, in 1570, was made commander of 5000 of the Tsar's men during the Polish War, and saw many scenes of horror (and Russian history is full of them), and later became Governor of Pskoff. It would be interesting to know more about his career.

Other Scots drifted into the Russian service and were continued in that of Ivan Groznie's son, the quiet Feodor. Giles Fletcher, writing in 1591, says 'of mercenarie soldiers that are strangers (whom they call *nemschoy*), they have at this time 4300 of Polonians: of Chircasses (that are under the Polonians) about four thousand, whereof 3500 are abroad in his garisons, of Deutches and Scots about 150, of Greekes, Turks, Danes, and Sweadens, all in one band an 100 or there abouts. But these they use only upon the Tartar side and against the Siberians.' They used Tartar levies against Poland and the West. These had all set allowances from what he calls the *Prechase shisivoy nemschoy*.[1]

[1] Fletcher's *The Russe Common Wealth*, pp. 52, 73.

The Scottish settlers, excluded like all heretics from the Kitai Gorod (China City) and the Byelo Gorod (White City) of Moscow, were placed in the Nemetskaya Sloboda,[1] 'the dumb suburb.'

The Russian word *nemetz*—originally meaning 'dumb'—was gradually applied to the 'dumb' inhabitants who knew little of Russian. In process of time it got to mean 'German,' but it included all the Protestant foreigners.[2]

The Scots married, as we have seen, with their fellow exiles, usually Livonians and Germans. One, a Hamilton,[3] almost certainly one of the Swedish prisoners, had in course of time, two descendants, sisters, both married to

[1] Situated 'beyond the gates of the old Capital, towards the north-western corner of the modern city, in the quarter lying between Basmannaïa Street and Pokrovskaïa Street, where at the present day most of the Protestant and Catholic churches stand.'—K. Waliszewski's *Peter the Great*, p. 15.

[2] R. Nisbet Bain's *The First Romanovs*, p. 122.

[3] The *Annuaire de la Noblesse de Russie*, 1889, tells us that the name became in Russia *Rehbinder*, 'singulière corruption du mot d'*Hamilton*, ancienne famille Anglaise (*sic*) arrivée en Russie déjà au commencement du XVIIe Siècle.' Helène Karlova de Rehbinder, died 1869, married Raphael Alexievitch Ostafieff. The name also became corrupted to Khomutoff.

Russians, one to Artamon Sergievitch Matveeff and the other Feodor Poleukhtovitch Narishkin,[1] names we shall hear again, as these marriages had a real bearing on Russian civilisation.

The gentle Tsar Feodor left but a slight mark on Russian history, save as the last of the Dynasty of Rurik, and when his wife's brother, Boris Feodorovitch Godounoff entered on the scene we find him much interested in foreigners. The English merchants believed in him thoroughly, but his rule was not long enough for them, and the end of his dynasty too swift. His successor, the False Dmitri (who claimed to be, and indeed perhaps was, the son of Ivan the Terrible by his seventh wife) had a Scot in his train whose history is instructive of the vicissitudes of Russia.

Captain David Gilbert, a Scot, had, with the Frenchman, Captain Margaret, and other international scoundrels, entered the service of the elected Tsar, Boris Godounoff. On his death he served in the bodyguard of the 'False

[1] *Story of Moscow*, by Wirt Gerrare, p. 121.

Dmitri, which (significant fact enough) was composed of foreigners. The bodyguard consisted of 300 English, French and Scots, divided into three squadrons, and commanded by officers of each nation.[1] He was one of the fifty-two strangers whom the second 'False Dmitri' wished to drown in the Oka on a sudden suspicion. These foreigners had already been driven from Koselsk towards Kaluga on the Oka, when Martin Beer, the chaplain, and Captain Gilbert, together with three others, Ensign Thomas Moritzen, and Reinhold von Engelhard and Johann von Reenen, two Livonian nobles, ventured to cross the river to implore and secure their pardon from Maryna Mniszek, through the medium of the ladies who were with her, to intercede for them. This Polish lady, the wife of the two successive pseudo-Dmitris, for she recognised both as husbands rather than give up her position of crowned Tsaritsa, therefore became the preserver of these 'innocent and [illegible] persons.' Gilbert subsequently

[1] Dr. Collins's *Present State of Russia* (French edition), p. 283.

served in the Polish ranks, but was soon taken prisoner and brought to Moscow. Sir John Merrick, who returned to England in 1617, then induced King James to intercede for him with the Tsar Michael Feodorovitch. Dr. Hamel writes: 'In the Tradescant (Ashmolean) Museum at Oxford I discovered the original dispatch from Michael Feodorovitch, which contains a reply to James, wherein Gilbert's great crime is circumstantially represented. By this it appears that on account of his desertion to the Poles, and the share he had taken in the many pillagings and blood sheddings at Moscow, and in the Empire generally, he had forfeited his life; but that at the King's request, he should be pardoned, and might return to his native country with Volunsky, the ambassador, who was dispatched to England in 1617. The above-named Russian dispatch (Gramota), discovered by me at Oxford, is much damaged. It is therein said, that in the letter from King James, delivered by Sir John Merrick, it was asserted that Gilbert was taken prisoner by Sholkevski's people, and

obliged to enter the Polish service, but that he was again taken prisoner by the Russians without having anywhere lent his assistance in injuring them, and that he had now been in fetters three years. The King requested that he might be set at liberty, and permission given him either to return to his native country or to enter in Russian service.' Gilbert had engaged to serve the Tsar Boris Feodorovitch, and under Vassili Shuiski. Then he had gone over to the second False Dmitri, and subsequently to the Poles. He came to Moscow with Zolkiewski (in the Polish army of Invasion), and was afterwards taken prisoner by the Russians while fighting against them. Dr. Hamel found, in 1836, among the MSS. of the Orusheinaya[1] Palace at Moscow that Gilbert, Captain Jacob Margaret, Robert Dunbar (another Scot), and Andrew Let (who had been recently baptised) were taken into the military service by Afanassi Ivanovitch Vlasseff in 1600-1601. Gilbert went to England, but returned to Russia with his son Thomas in one of the Tradescant ships in

[1] Dr. J. Hamel, *England and Russia*, 1854, pp. 402-407.

1618. 'During his stay in England,' says Dr. Hamel, 'Captain Gilbert gave some account of the first Pretender Demetrius. According to him, Demetrius, a few days before his end, and consequently very soon after his nuptials[1] (for between both events but nine days intervened), saw two apparitions in the night, which so much disturbed him that he first came to Gilbert in the ante-room, where his life-guards were, and then sent for Butschinski, his private secretary.

'Gilbert likewise related in England that he received from the second Pretender Demetrius a written invitation, in which the writing of the first usurper was imitated. When Gilbert approached him with his guards he displayed so accurate a knowledge of all the affairs of the first Pretender that ... he should have believed in the identity of the one with the other ... if

[1] To Maryna, daughter of George Mniszek, Palatin of Sandomir. The False Demetrius married her at Moscow on May 9, 1606, and she was then crowned Tsaritza. Demetrius was killed on May 17th by being thrown from the window of his palace in the Kremlin by the conspirators. The way another was able to claim his pretensions was that his mangled body was shown to the crowd of rioters masked.

he had not been personally so well acquainted with the first.' The first Dmitri was, he said, a man of 'very prepossessing exterior,' while the second (who *bien entendu* wished to drown Gilbert in the Oka) was 'a very deformed wretch,' quite different. He said, too, he had spoken to the Polish Hetman Ruskinski of this difference, but received the answer, 'It is no matter, Captaine, this Demetrius shall serve our turne to be revenged of the —— Russe.'

In 1610[1] another Scot, Captain Robert Carr, accompanied Gilbert and his son to Russia. He commanded one of the six companies of British cavalry which on June 24, 1610, remained for the longest time on the battlefield in the defeat of the new Tsar Vassili Shuiski's army by the Poles at Kluchino under the Grand Hetman Zolkiewski. He there lost his whole company, but remained unwounded. The names of the other captains were Benson, Crale, Creyton (Crichton), Kendrick and York. Young Thomas Gilbert and Captain

[1] Hamel says 1618—no doubt a misprint.

Carr[1] returned to England in 1619, but Captain David Gilbert remained in Russia and most likely died there.

[1] He may have returned to Russia. At least a noble Russian family Kar (among the many noble families, like the family of the Bestucheffs—from Best, an Englishman—of foreign origin), originally like the Bruces 'from North Britain,' is mentioned by William Tooke in his *View of the Russian Empire during the Reign of Catherine the Second* (London, 1799).

CHAPTER III.

THE FIRST ROMANOFFS. MICHAEL FEODOROVITCH. HIS SON ALEKSEI MICHAELOVITCH. REFUSES TO RECOGNISE CROMWELL. INFLUX OF ROYALIST SCOTS. THE TSAR'S MARRIAGE TO NATALIA NARISHKINA, NIECE OF A HAMILTON.

III.

After the quick change of Tsars, the Godounoffs, 'false Dmitris,' the Shuiskis, and the rapine and murder that came in their train, it was a mercy for Russia that, by what passed at that date for the will of the people, the first Tsar of the new Dynasty, Michael Feodorovitch Romanoff, was elected. The Romanoff family stood high in popular estimation. They were descended in the female line from the Princes of Susdal of the blood of Rurik, connected by marriage both with the old Dynasty of Rurik and the newer one of Godounoff. More than all, the new Tsar was an amiable young man, soon to be supported by the guidance of his father, the Patriarch Philarete, and already by that of his mother, the astute Nun Marfa, in the world, Ksenia Ivanovna Shestova. He was summoned to the throne in March, 1613, and a stable Dynasty was once more established.[1] To have a better army was his first thought, and the fear of another Polish war forced him to send for foreign mercenaries to teach the native levies European methods. In 1614 foreign soldiers began to pour into Russia, preferably from Protestant countries, for the Orthodox Church looked askance at Catholics on account of their Polish sympathies. Still, in 1624 we note in the Russian service 445 foreign officers, 168 Poles, 113 'Germans,' who probably included the Scottish officers, Leslie, Keith and Matthison, and the Englishmen, Fox and Sanderson, and sixty-four Irish. Tsar Michael's army, says Dr. Nisbet Bain,[2] 'was an improvement upon all previous Moscovite armies, but when it came to be tested in the Second Polish War, the

[1] Even in the time of the Troubles trade must have continued with the West. In 1614 Jean Ruthven writes from Whitehall to Anna, Countess of Eglinton, about a 'bowat' or lantern. 'The casements of it is not of horne but of Moscovia glas, such a thing as will nether bow nor brek easily.'—*Historical MSS. Commission Reports, the Earl of Eglinton's MSS.*, p. 43.

[2] R. Nisbet Bain, *The First Romanovs*, p. 57.

chief event of Michael's later years, its inadequacy was most painfully demonstrated.'

In 1631, when the first Romanoff reigned, a Scot, Sir Alexander Leslie of Auchintoul, arrived in Russia with a letter from King Charles I. to the Tsar Michael. The Patriarch Philarete, then co-regent, sent him to Sweden to hire 5000 infantry, and persuade smiths and wheelwrights, carpenters, etc., to come to Russia. He was successful, and by the end of 1631 there were 66,000 mercenaries in Moscow.[1] Another Scot, Captain William Gordon, was at the same time in the Muscovite service, and in 1634, a Lieutenant-Colonel Alexander Gordon. He appears in Sir Thomas Urquhart's 'Jewel' among the 'Scottish Colonels that served under the great Duke of Muscovy, against the Tartar and Polonian.' Among Sir Thomas Urquhart's Scots was another, 'Colonel Thomas Garne, agnamed the Sclavonian and upright Gentile, who, for the height and grossness of his person, being in his stature taller, and greater in his compass

[1] R. Nisbet Bain's *Slavonic Europe*, pp. 194-195.

of body than any within six kingdoms about him, was elected King of Bucharia,' a statement that we feel still needs verification!

In the reign of the next Tsar, Aleksei Michaelovitch (1645-1676), we find a marked increase in Scottish influence in Russia. He it was, and not his greater son, who first saw the necessity of more foreign soldiers. Two regiments, 'one of cavalry and one of infantry, were commanded by a Scotsman as Colonel, and have a staff's company in each of them. He received four times the usual pay.'[1] This Scot was probably Sir Alexander Leslie of Auchintoul, already mentioned as in the Russian service. On 28th March, 1633, Captain James Forbes had had a Royal Letter to allow him to raise in Scotland 200 men for the Russian service under Sir Alexander Leslie, and on 1st May, 1633, a warrant to levy the same number of men for Sir Alexander Leslie, Knight, 'Generall Colonel of the Forrain forces of the Emperour of Russia,'[2] was

[1] Tooke's *View of the Russian Empire*, p. 474.

[2] *Register of the Privy Council of Scotland*, vol. v. 2nd series, pp. 79, 548.

granted, and though the Parliamentary Wars broke out soon, there is no doubt many Scots went to Russia and into the Russian Army.

The new Tsar sent an ambassador, Docturoff (Gerasimus), to England to inform King Charles I. of his accession. The troubles were far afield by that time, and Parliament, which offered to receive his credentials, was spurned by him. In May, 1646, when he heard that the King had surrendered to the Parliament, the Russian again demanded an audience. Eventually he was presented to both Houses, but he still refused to present his credentials to anyone but the King. In consequence of his report the Tsar rescinded the privileges of the English merchants in Russia, and, when news arrived of the execution of Charles I., Aleksei issued a *Ukase* forbidding them residence in his Empire. 'At the request of your sovereign, King Charles, and because of our brotherly love and friendship towards him,' he wrote, 'you were allowed to trade with us by virtue of letters of commerce, but it has been made known to us that you English have done a great wickedness by killing your sovereign, King Charles, for which evil deed you cannot be suffered to remain in the realm of Muscovy.'[1] This did not affect the Scots, whom the Tsar welcomed from their loyalty. Cromwell he abhorred, and with him he had 'no dealings,' so the exiles who upheld the Stuart cause were welcomed with open arms.

In 1656 Thomas Dalyell of Binns, who never shaved his beard after the execution of his beloved master, King Charles I., and another loyalist, William Drummond of Cromlix, entered the Russian service together. The former became a General, and the latter a Lieutenant-General, and both returned to Scotland (only permitted to do so by the Tsar at the direct entreaty of King Charles II.) in 1665. The autocratic rule they bore over their men was noticed by the unfortunate Covenanters after their return home. Kirkton[2] wrote of Dalyell as a man whose 'rude and fierce natural disposition hade been much

[1] R. Nisbet Bain, *The First Romanovs*, p. 98.

[2] *History of the Church of Scotland*, p. 225.

confirmed by his breeding and service in Muscovia, where he hade the command of a small army and saw nothing but tyrranie and slavery;' while Bishop Burnet wrote of 'Drumond' that he 'had yet too much of the air of Russia about him, though not with Dalziel's fierceness.' Dalyell was also denounced as 'a Muscovia beast who used to roast men,' and accused of having, with General Drummond, 'who had seen it in Muscovia,' introduced the playful torture of the 'thummikins' or thumbscrews into Scotland, though Lord Fountainhall[1] has to point out that it was already known there, though called by 'another name,' *i.e.* 'the pilliewincks.' These two Generals were 'noblie entertained' by the Tsar, and Drummond became Governor of Smolensk. He was created, in 1686, Viscount Strathallan, and Dalyell died at Edinburgh in August, 1685.

One must note also Paul Menezius, a son of Sir Gilbert Menzies of Pitfoddels, who came to Russia from the Polish service in 1661, with Patrick Gordon. The Tsar Aleksei at once

[1] *Historical Notices of Scottish Affairs*, i. p. 32, ii. p. 557.

singled him out and matched him to a Russian wife, and in 1661-2, he became (as we shall see) a member of the suite of the Boyar Feodor Michaelovitch Milotawski, envoy to Persia. In 1672 he acted as the Tsar's envoy to Prussia and to Vienna to propose a league against the Turk. He proceeded to Rome to petition Pope Clement X. to assist Poland against the Sultan, and brought off his mission (which involved the question of the full obeisance as an equivalent of kissing the Pope's slipper and other difficult questions) with dignity. He returned from his mission in 1674, and advanced in rank. He is said to have been tutor to Peter the Great until 1682, when the Regent, Princess Sophia, sent him to Smolensk, and made him take part, in 1689, in the war against the Tartars of the Crimea. The Narishkins called him back to Moscow in that year, where he died, a Lieutenant-General, 9th November, 1694, leaving a wife and children.[1] Several of

[1] As a faithful Catholic and a good Scot, he, when at Rome, obtained from Pope Clement X. the permission for a service commemorating Saint Margaret, Queen of Scotland. (See also Chapters IV., V.)

the Catholic family of Menzies tried their fortune in Russia under the hospitable Tsar; Lieutenant-Colonel Thomas Menzies of Balgownie was another. He married at Riga in July, 1651, 'the Ladie Marie Farserson, borne of noble and honourable parentage in the dukedome of Curland,' and was wounded and taken prisoner by his countryman, Lord Henry Gordon (fighting for the Poles), at Szudna, in 1660. We are told that he 'dyed of his woundes in Ukraine, and was buried in the fields at Szudna.' We shall see that his widow remarried, in 1661, Ruitmaster Ryter at Moscow.[1]

Sir Alexander Leslie of Auchintoul, who, as we have seen, was the chief of the permanent foreign legion, remained in Russia, and did not return to Scotland to die, like Generals Dalyell and Drummond. He became 'a Colonel there under the Great Duke of Musco' and 'had a son there called Theodorus.'[2] He was made

[1] He is also styled Sir William Reuter. By her first husband she had three sons, Thomas Alexander, who died young at Riga, John Ledowick, and William, both living in February, 1672.

[2] Macfarlane's *Genealogical Collections* (Scottish History Society), vol. i. p. 66.

General and Governor of Smolensk, and died in 1661 at the great age of ninety-five. Two other Leslies, probably basking in his great favour, Alexander (a son of Kininvie) who 'died sans Issue being a Captain,' and a Leslie of Wardis, were in Russia about the same time, as well as George Leslie, a Capuchin at Archangel.

It is pleasant to be able to reconstruct a little the *coterie* of Sir Alexander Leslie of Auchintoul from the demands for 'Birthbrieves,' which some of his brothers-in-arms desired and obtained to prove their nobility. In 1636 (13th October) the Privy Council of Scotland[1] allowed 'Colonel John Kynninmonth, Governor of Nettenburg in Russia,' of an adventurous family who had an offshoot also in Sweden, to have his 'Certificat of his lawful birth and progenie . . . exped under the Great Seal.'

The Keith family,—to distinguish themselves in Russia so greatly,—sent an offshoot there early. One 'Lieutenant George Keith, who did serve under the Lord of . . . as levtenent Colonell

[1] *Reg.* vi. 2nd series, p. 327.

in Ireland and is now certanely informit to be departit this lyff in Muscovia some yeirs ago.'[1] He left an heir, Alexander Keith, who claimed,[2] 8th July, 1662, under the guardianship of his mother's brother, Sir Alexander Keith of Ludquharn, to be 'only lawful son' of Major William Keith, only son of Robert Keith of Kindruct, eldest brother of the Russian soldier. Perhaps the latter's widow or daughter (forgotten by or not known to her Scottish relatives) was the Juliana Keith whose marriage in the Moscow *Sloboda* of the Strangers we shall find witnessed by Patrick Gordon.

There is also a petition for a 'borebreiff' from Lieutenant-Colonel Alexander Hamilton, who thought that a deed under 'the great seall' would 'clear his descent,' and got it, 1st March, 1670. He was eldest son of Sir Alexander

[1] Perhaps this Keith sent home the picture which belonged to Mary, Countess Marischal (wife of the head of the Keith family) at the House of Fetteresso, 25th October, 1722, and was marked in her Inventory as 'The Czar of Moscovie.'—*The Lords Elphinstone of Elphinstone*, by Sir William Fraser, K.C.B., vol. ii. p. 274.

[2] *Birthbrieves from the Registers of the Burgh of Aberdeen* (Spalding Club Miscellany), viii. p. 340.

Hamilton of Fenton and Innerwick in East Lothian, and is stated[1] to have left no issue.

We notice that in 1665 'ane Kenedy,' a Scot, was at Moscow apparently connected with medicine, as he was with the English doctor who 'lodged by Dr. Collins,' the Tsar's physician, who published, in 1671, an excellent and rare book on "The Present State of Russia." Kennedy was entrusted with letters to Scotland,[2] but they never reached there, as he (though he lived after) 'had a fitt of a frensy' at Riga.

It is also quite possible that Christopher Galloway, the 'English clockmaker,' who went out to the Court of the Tsar Michael Feodorovitch, and was later the architect of the Tower of the Troitski Gate of the Kremlin in Moscow, built early in the seventeenth century, was from North Britain, as his name would seem to indicate.

We have already mentioned the marriages of two sisters, Hamiltons, of the *Slobóda*, one to

[1] Douglas, *Baronage of Scotland*, vol. i. p. 462.

[2] Diary of Patrick Gordon, p. 69.

Artamon Sergievitch Matveeff, the Tsar's favourite and chief Boyar, and the other to Feodor Poleukhtovitch Narishkin. These had a marked effect on the position of the Scots, and in the following way. There lived, it is said, much with Matveeff and his Scottish wife,[1] her sister's niece, Nathalia Kirillovna Narishkina, a pretty Russian *Barinia*. Madame Matveeva educated her according to the free manner of the Scots, allowing her to receive male visitors, a practice horrible to the cloistered seclusion of the women of the Russian *Terem*. After the death, in 1669, of his first wife, Maria Ileinishna Miloslavskaya, the Tsar, Aleksei Michaelovitch, seeking distraction, went to see his familiar friend Matveeff, and in his house met his *protegée*. Attracted by the girl, he first promised her a husband, and then demanded her in marriage. Matveeff, frightened at the

[1] Dr. Collins, the Tsar's English Physician, however, says that the Grand Master of the Court, 'Bogdan Batfeidg's' fondness for Polish girls made his wife so jealous that he had her poisoned and that he had heard he was about to marry a former love. Perhaps this was his second wife. He adds 'He did not love the English, having been gained over by the Dutch, by presents.'

honour, and more especially at the un-Byzantine way the lovers had met, begged the Tsar to reconsider his decision. A *via media* was found. The Byzantine 'choice of brides' was summoned. Sixty Boyars' daughters came to the Tsar's call, and then, as may be imagined, the middle-aged Tsar made choice of Nathalia and wedded her on 21st January, 1672.

Nathalia Narishkina thus became mother of Peter the Great, and though she did not do anything extraordinary herself for the Westernisation of Russia, she undoubtedly instilled the desire for it into the great brain of her son. Her influence with her husband was considerable. She was allowed to go unveiled, and, once at least, to 'receive,' and—unheard of innova tion—to drive in an open coach or litter; and owing to her influence, he, who began his reign with religious discussions and persecution of sorcerers, ended it by seeing the first theatrical performances in Moscow.

CHAPTER IV.

GENERAL PATRICK GORDO
AUCHLEUCHRIES.

esolved, I say, to go to some
, not careing much on what
which country I should go,
nowne ffriend in any foreigne
'on his own,' he sailed to
tertained by Scots (of whom
ıy), thought of becoming a
erg, 'yet could not my humer
still and strict way of liveing.'
hips from poverty and adven-
erty always sends, he was be-
ttish merchants at Danzig and
a countryman and namesake'
d the Scots not go?) at Culm,
on by more Scots to Poland,
Ian Radzewill had a lyfe com-
ost Scottismen,' but at Posen
ained by kindly Scottish mer-
ntually entered into the suite of
, Opalinski, who was travelling
ith him he went to Antwerp.
as enticed by a 'ruitmaster' of
n (with the help of some wine)
Swedish army in 1655, and the

same year was in Prussia and Poland, the war with the latter country having begun again. Here he received his baptism of fire, having a horse killed under him and being shot in the leg. Then he was, in 1656, captured by the Poles. He was liberated only on the condition that he would join the Polish army, and as a Catholic he probably preferred it to that of the Swedes, into which he had been enticed, so he became a dragoon under Constantine Lubomirski, Starost of Sandets. Captured by the Swedes, he again served under them, and helped to plunder the unhappy country of East Prussia. His life was passed in being captured and re-captured, at one time by the Poles and in 1657 by the Imperial Forces. After much plundering and fighting and changes of masters, he was, in 1661, thinking of joining the Imperial Service, when at Warsaw he received an offer to join that of Russia from the 'Russe ambassador, Zamiati Feodorovitz Leontieff and Colonell Crawfuird' (Daniel Crawfurd, son of Hew Crawfurd of Jordanhill[1]), who had been

[1] He was Governor of Smolensk, and 'died Governor of

taken prisoner from the Russian service. He set out with Colonel Crawfurd, Captain Paul Menzies and five servants for the Russia in which he ended his days, not without much misgiving. At Riga he began engaging good officers for the Tsar's service. He got two old Scottish friends, Alexander Landells and Walter Airth to join. This was not so difficult as it seemed, as the soldiers of the Swedes, miserably paid, lived by plunder, and they 'heard that the Moskovites' pay, though not great, was duly payed, and that officers were soone advanced to high charges; that many of our countreymen of great quality were there, and some gone thither lately.' At Plesko, or Opsko, and there 'one William Hay, who was lately come from Scotland, came to us and made one of our company to Mosco,' a John Hamilton also joined them. On September 2 he enters in his journal: 'Wee came to Mosko and hired a lodging in the Slabod or village

[illegible] His elder brother, [illegible] Crawfurd, was a Colonel in the 'Muscovite service, and married a daughter of Colonel Alexander Crawfurd, but died *anno* 1685, without surviving issue.'—Douglas's *Baronage of Scotland*, p. 430.

where the strangers live,' and three days later they 'were admitted to kiss his Tzaarsky Majestie's hand at Columinske,[1] a countrey house of the Tzaars, seven wersts from Mosko. . . The Tzaar was pleased to thank me for haveing been kind to his subjects who were prisoners in Polland; and it was told me that I should have his Majestie's Grace or favour, wherein I might rely.' The father of the Tsar's first wife 'Elia (Ilia) Danillovitz Miloslavsky,' had 'the command of the Stranger Office,' saw the strangers drill, and Gordon 'handled the pike and musket, with all their postures, to his great satisfaction.' Having once got into Russia, Gordon and his Scottish friends found that they had to make the best of a bad bargain, as they began to fear it was. The copper coin was adulterated. Nor was Gordon pleased with the attitude of the Russians towards their foreign legion. 'Strangers' he perceived 'to be looked upon as a company of hirelings, and, at the [illegible] (as they say at

[1] Kolomenskye; about ten versts from Moscow, on the River Moskva.

woman) but *necessaria mala*; no honours or degrees of preferment to be expected here but military, and that with a limited command, no marrying with natives, strangers being looked upon by the best sort as scarcely Christians, and by the plebeyans as meer pagans, and the worst of all' (here speaks the Scot) 'the pay small.' He tried to get leave, but exile to Siberia was hinted at, so rather reluctantly he remained and was given a regiment which he officered with his countrymen; those already named, besides William Guild, George Keith, Andrew Burnet, Andrew Calderwood, Robert Stuart, 'and others,' about thirty in all, mostly collected in Riga. Disgusted at the suspicion of the Russians, Gordon tried to join the embassy of Feodor Michaelovitch Milotawski to Persia, but this was not permitted, though his friend, Captain Paul Menzies, obtained the post by a gift of a hundred ducats to the Boyar and a saddle and bridle worth twenty ducats to his steward, and Gordon was given the rank of Lieutenant-Colonel in 1662, and resolved to marry.

but the following summer resolved to dispatch him on a mission to the King of England, as no Russian boyar at the time, 'fearing such cold entertainment as Diascow (Vassili Jakolevitch Dashkoff) had got,' was willing to go. On his way to England another Scot, one Captain Peter Rae, was of his suite, and at Pskoff he met another 'M'Naughton.' Once in England he had much communication with his *confrères*, Generals Dalyell and Drummond, who had also been in the Muscovite service, and had the satisfaction of an interview with King Charles II., for—utilitarian in allegiance as he was abroad—Gordon was a devoted adherent of the Stuarts at home. The King had a servant, one Gaspar Kalthoff, or Calthoffe, detained in Russia with the 'hospitality' of the Russians of those times, whose release he wished and which he asked Gordon to obtain. He bore a letter from the King to the Tsar (wishing for the restoration of the 'Privilydges' of the English merchants) when he returned to Russia in 1667. We notice incidentally that amongst his correspondents were

He returned to Tschigirin, and had again to defend it against an attack of the Grand Vizier Kara Mustapha. He took the command, when the Governor was killed by a bomb, and the campaign ended in the slaughter of four thousand Turks, a complete victory, and the position of Major-General.

In 1679 he was appointed to the Chief Command at Kiev, and in 1683 was made Lieutenant-General, and in that year (the Tsar Feodor had died in 1683, succeeded by his two brothers Ivan and Peter, with the Tsarevna Sophia as Regent), hungering after Moscow, he travelled thither. Well received by Sophia, he was again sent back to Kiev, and fortified it against a Turkish invasion. He there met the Genevan adventurer, Francis Lefort, the friend of Peter the Great, who became connected with him by marriage, and their friendship endured for life.

At the end of the year he lost a son, George Stephen Gordon, and wrote a Latin epitaph on him; he also commemorated another Scot (how many were there in Russia?), one Andrew

the Boyar,[1] who desired me to returne speedily and not to drowne him my cautioner.' Truly foreigners in the service of Russia had uneasy heads! He visited England, was received and well received by King James II. and Queen Marie, and then revisited Scotland, his native land. Armed with letters from his King and the Duke of Gordon (head of his family), begging the Tsars and Prince Galitzin to give him his *congé* and let him enjoy his estates in Scotland, to which he had now succeeded, he returned to Russia at the end of the year. He again found himself in slight disgrace, but in January of next year he was told he was to serve against the Tartars of the Crimea, and he received the rank of General in September, 1687. In 1688 he had trouble on account of the Patriarch prophesying that the Muscovites could not thrive while a heretic commanded their best soldiers. He began, however, to grow in favour with the Boyars, and especially with the young Tsar Peter.

[1] Prince Vassili Vassilievitch Galitzin, the married favourite of the Regent, the Tsarevna Sophia.

In May, 1689, after an abortive expedition against the Crimean Tartars, the Tsar Peter accorded him the special privilege of being addressed in the third person, and also as Patrick Ivanovitch, like a genuine Russian. On August 6 he notes there were 'rumours unsafe to be uttered,' and next day the Tsar Peter fled for safety to Troitza. Gordon[1] threw in his lot with him, though not till after he had consulted Prince Galitzin. He joined the Tsar at the Troitskaya Lavra, 60 versts from Moscow, with his troops, and was admitted as a friend. They returned to Moscow triumphantly, the Tsarevna Sophia was sent to a convent, and much blood spilt, and (the Tsar Ivan being passive) the Tsar Peter became sole ruler.

Gordon was now frequently at Court with the young Tsar (we must note that when his mother-in-law died he could not appear before the Tsar for three days, as he had been at a funeral!) and frequently was honoured with gifts, and was, owing to his knowledge of

[1] Gordon drew up the note of his services in Russia, which ended with his going to the monastery of the Troitza. *Diary*, p. 172.

In 1693, the Tsar showered favours on Gordon after his first visit to Archangel, and after the Tsaritza-dowager's death, was supported by Gordon, who acted as Rear-Admiral of the Fleet, on his second visit to Archangel next year. In 1695 there was an attack planned on Azof, one fort of which was stormed by Colonel James Gordon, but it was not till 1696 that it was finally taken by the Russians. The only officer of distinction the Russians lost was Colonel Stevenson, 'a Scots gentleman' who was 'shot in the mouth being a little too curious, and raising himself too high on the top of the loose earth to observe the enemy,' whom the Tsar buried 'with all the honours of war.' On the return of the triumphant troops to Moscow in October, Gordon received a medal worth six ducats, a gold cup, a sable robe and an estate with ninety souls. When the reforming Tsar set out on his travels he continued to correspond with Gordon from London, and Gordon replied telling him of the unrest among the Streltzi; and when the storm of mutiny broke out among the regiments Gordon surrounded them and fired putting the Zarina in the Convent.' But Gordon was not long to enjoy the Imperial favour. He was able to see 'the crocodile, swordfish, and other curiosities, which his Majesty had brought from England and Holland' on September 30th, but in December of 1698 he entered: 'This year I have felt a sensible decrease of health and strength. Yet Thy will be done, Gracious God!' He lingered for another year, visited by the Tsar, who stood weeping by his bedside, at his deathbed. The Tsar ordered his funeral procession, which was military. Two Generals supported the widow, and twenty Boyarinas walked in her train. He was buried before the high altar in the first stone church the Roman Catholics were allowed to build in Moscow, which he had assisted in building, and the inscription on his tomb read:

SACRAE TZAREAE MAJESTATIS MILITIAE GENERALIS
PATRICIUS LEOPOLDUS GORDON
NATUS ANNO DOMINI 1635 DIE 31 MARTII
DENATUS ANNO DOMINI 1699 DIE 29 NOVEMBRIS
REQUIESCAT IN PACE.

General Gordon was twice married: first, as we have seen, to Katherine von Bockhoven, and fell a victim in 1692 (by an explosion) to Peter the Great's love for fireworks. In 1700 she remarried Alexander Gordon of Auchintoul (of whom we shall hear later), and left Russia with him in 1711. She died in Scotland in 1739. The second daughter, Marie, married a Scot, Major Daniel Crawford (who also died in 1692, in the Tsar's service), and the Tsar was present at the wedding. She remarried Colonel Carl Snivius, probably a German of the Sloboda.

The mantle of Gordon fell, in a measure, on his (future) son-in-law, Alexander Gordon of Auchintoul,[1] called in Russia Aleksei Alexandrovitch. Originally in the French Army, he came to Moscow in 1696, and was made Major in Gordon's regiment. He was at the capture of Azof, and became a Major-General of the Russian service. Returning to Scotland, he was 'out' in the '15' but escaped attainder as a Jacobite by a mistake in the Act. He lived until 1751; having remarried in 1740 Margaret,

[1] For a full account of his services, see J. M. Bullough's excellent *House of Gordon*, pp. 412-5 (New Spalding Club).

CHAPTER VI.

COLLABORATORS OF PETER THE GREAT.

him that (through the influence of the un-
unate Livonian Count Patkul) he took him
his service, and they went back to Moscow
ether. After General Lefort's death Ogilvy
s made Field-Marshal. 'His first care was
arrange Military matters according to German
le, and in this he succeeded very well,' but
was wise enough to see and to say that the
ssians were but in their infancy, and ought
be brought into discipline by degrees. He
tinguished himself at the taking of Narva,
d concluded the Peace of Ivanogorod, when
e King of Poland decorated him with the
hite Eagle. With the Tsar's permission he
en took service with the King of Poland, and
ed in October, 1710, aged sixty-two, at
anzig. He bought for 120,000 florins the
udal estate of Sauershau, and (by his wife,
larie-Anastasia, daughter of Johann Georg
uckmantel de Brümath) left a family to
ucceed him in the riches he had acquired in
ussia.[1]

[1] A pedigree of his descendants is given in *The Scottish ntiquary.*

Major-General James Daniel (Yakov Vilemovitch, 1670-1735) Bruce and his brother, Robert (Roman Vilemovitch, 1668-1720), were sons of an immigrant to Russia, Colonel William Bruce,[1] who claimed to belong to the old house of Bruce of Airth.[2] They prospered exceedingly in the land of their adoption. We are told of James Bruce that he 'passed at Court for a chemist and astronomer of genius, and was held in the City for a Sorcerer.' He certainly was one of the greatest of the Tsar Peter's 'helpers.' There was nothing he had not a finger in. He was placed at the head of the artillery and was not unsuspected of much peculation. His career was subject to sudden vicissitudes. He was at one time disgraced in favour of Prince Ivan Troubetskoi for 'lack of expedition,' and at another time for abuses in his office, though he had the reputation of never accepting bribes.

[1] *A Short Outline of the History of Russia*, by B. I. L. (Edinburgh: privately printed, 1900), p. 119. A book too little known. William Bruce is said to have arrived in Russia about 1650. He died in 1680 at Pskoff.

[2] See chapter vii.

The Tsar always ended by forgiving him. He had the great power of work, which was after the great Tsar's heart, and his success at the Peace of Nystadt, which gave him the title of Count, gave the Baltic Provinces to Russia, and left Sweden with no transmaritime possessions. He also induced Peter to correspond with Leibnitz, translated many foreign books for his master, and directed the Tsar's schools of Navigation, Artillery and Military Engineering. It was he who was made to collect codes of laws of other nations for the Tsar, and he was made a Senator in 1718. He later retired to his estate of Glinki, forty-two versts from Moscow, and died without issue, 19th April, 1735. Waliszewski[1] writes: 'A whole legend has grown up round the light which streamed, on long winter nights, from the windows of his laboratory in the Souharef Tower.[2] His astronomical discoveries bordered

[1] *Peter the Great*, p. 226. A bust (lettered additionally Daniel Bruce) which has disappeared since his birth [illegible]. I am indebted for its photograph to my friend, Mr. Clement J. Charnock, of Moscow.

[2] *Souchareva bashnya.*

closely on Astrology, and his celebrated *Calendar*, published in 1711, is all moonshine.'[1] Brusovski Street in Moscow, where his house formerly stood, is named after him. His Countship passed on to his nephew, Alexander Romanovitch, the son of his brother, Robert (Roman), who was born in 1705. He took part in the war with the Turks, and was a Major-General by 1739. He retired, owing to ill-health, in 1751, and died the same year. He married twice into the family of Dolgorouki. His first wife was Princess Anastasia Michaelovna Dolgoroukaya; secondly, he married a lady who had almost been Tsaritza of Russia, Princess Yekaterina Aleksievna Dolgoroukaya, the bereaved *fiancée* of the young Tsar, Peter II., who was described as 'beautiful, but arrogant.' On the death of her *fiancé* she was (by Anna Ivanovna) banished and confined in different monasteries, but when the Empress Elizabeth came to the throne she was recalled in [illegible]. It was noticed that her hand had

[1] Field-Marshal Bruce lies buried under the Refectory of the Simonoff Monastery in Moscow.—*The Story of Moscow*, by Writ Gerrare, p. 262.

been kissed by the Empress when she was declared the Tsar's *fiancée*. We are told that, 'Arrogant till the very last, on her death-bed she ordered all her dresses to be burned so that none might wear them after her.'[1] Her stepson was one of the 'Counts Bruce' of the reign of Catherine II.

Dr. Robert Erskine, the sixth son of Sir Charles Erskine of Alva, Baronet, a Scottish physician who had studied in Paris, entered the service of Peter the Great and became the first of the many Scottish physicians connected with the Russian Court. Perhaps he originally took service with Prince Menschikoff, the Tsar's favourite, but anyway he entered the Tsar's service about 1704. He was appointed *Archiator* or chief of the *Aptekarski Prikaz*, or Ministry of Medical Affairs, which was removed in 1712 from Moscow to the new St. Petersburg, when the name was changed to that of Medical Chancellery, and he was used in diplomatic missions also with Tartar Khans. We are told he had the salary of 1500 ducats

[1] *Short Outline of the History of Russia*, ii. pp. 152-3.

(promptly paid too, unlike the military allowances), and that he 'put the great Imperial Dispensary in the excellent order it is in.... He furnishes the armies and fleets, and the whole Empire, with drugs, and makes a great addition to the Tsar's revenue.'[1]

It is interesting to see how a Scottish friend, George Mackenzie, describes in a letter the newly-born St. Petersburg in 1714. 'Our infant City here is of that extent, that, though far from being at the fag end of it, yet have my house at above 2 English miles distance from that of the Dr.'s, so that my letter found him allready gone abroad with the Czar, though it was with him this morning before 7 o'clock.'

Erskine rose high in the opinion of his Imperial Patron, travelled with him and Catherine in 1716 through Denmark, Germany and Holland. He was given the title of Councillor of State. He was present at the marriage of the Tsar's niece, the Tsarevna Yekaterina Ivanovna (mother of the unlucky

[1] *History of Peter the Great*, 1755, ii. pp. 170-171.

Regent, Anna Leopoldovna), to the Duke of Mecklenburg-Schwerin, at Danzig on 19th April, 1716. At Copenhagen he was approached by the Jacobites (his brother was one of those attainted in 1715), and Sir Henry Stirling of Ardoch (son-in-law of Admiral Thomas Gordon), came to meet him there, no doubt as a Jacobite agent, and he was very likely in the Görtz plot; anyhow, as Gordon of Auchintoul wrote: 'The Doctor was supposed in the latter years of his life to have kept a correspondence with the Chevalier de St. George's agents; whatever be of that, he was an agreeable, open-hearted, fine gentleman.' In spite, or because of this (for the Tsar did *not* love George I.), his influence continued unabated. He went with him on the celebrated visit to Paris in 1717. Next year he fell ill and went for baths at Koucheserski, near Lake Onega, and died at the Tsar's house there in December, 1718. He was only forty-one. The Tsar had his body transported to the capital, and had it buried in the churchyard of the newly-erected Alexander Nevski Monastery

with the highest pomp. The funeral took place on 4th January, 1719, the Tsar carrying a lighted torch, with two hundred other mourners.[1]

Always well treated by the Tsar and handsomely paid, he returned the Imperial kindness in his will, dated in 1718. He left all his money in England to his mother, that in Russia to necessitous families. His library was to be sold for the benefit of his heirs. If the Tsar liked he could purchase his curiosities, medals and surgical instruments, the price being given to orphanages, hospitals, and almshouses in Scotland. Two legacies he made to the Imperial family, and both are characteristic of the time and country. He leaves 'To the Most Gracious Lady the Tsaritsa Ekaterina Aleksievna such of my linen as has not been used, and the lace which is not torn, and all my porcelain ware,' and 'The Country seat Gastel (now called Gostilitzi) I transfer to the most gracious pleasure of His Imperial Majesty, in case he should wish to give it to her Highness

[1] Erskine Papers; *Miscellany of the Scottish History Society*, vol. ii. pp. 373-430.

the eldest Princess.'[1] We read, also, among his papers a letter in 1713 desiring a recommendation to him of 'Thomas Garvine, who is now a surgeon in the Hospital of Petersburg,' and who was sent later by Peter the Great to Peking at the request of the Chinese Emperor, Kang Hi, on one of those Oriental missions which owed so much to Scottish leaders.

Such was the career of the first, but by no means the last,[2] Scottish Court Physician in Russia.

John Bell of Antermony, whose name is associated with diplomatic relations between Russia and China, went to Russia in 1714, and was received by Dr. Erskine 'in a very friendly manner.' Desiring to travel, Dr. Erskine recommended him, as having some knowledge of surgery, to the College of Foreign Affairs in St. Petersburg, and so he entered the Tsar's service.

[1] Anna Petrovna, born 9th March, 1708; died 15th May, 1728; married, 1725, Charles, Duke of Holstein-Gottorp and was mother of Peter III.

[2] Dr. Grieve was later another Scottish doctor in St. Petersburg, also Dr. Halliday, who died there in the beginning of the eighteenth century.—*New Statistical Account of Scotland (Dumfriesshire)*, p. 156.

He first went in the suite of Artemy Petrovitch Valenski on the embassy from 'his Czarish' Majesty to the Sophy of Persia, which lasted from 1715 to 1718, and next year set off in the train of Leoff Vassilievitch Ismayloff, ambassador from the Tsar to Kang Hi, Emperor of China. Two excellent volumes, published by subscription later, were the fruit of his observations. His Chinese embassy did not reach home until 1721. It was a great success, and may be studied in his book.[1] It is sad to read how many prisoners (one a General Hamilton),[2] taken in the Swedish wars, he met going and returning through Kazan and Siberia; though he states that in the case of the latter they 'contributed not a little to the civilizing of the inhabitants of these distant regions; as they were the means of introducing several useful

[1] *Travels from St. Petersburg in Russia to Diverse Parts of Asia*, 2 vols. (Glasgow, 1763.) A good life is given in W. Anderson's *Scottish Nation*, vol. ii. pp. 273-275.

[2] Hugo Johan Hamilton, Major-General of the Swedish cavalry, was taken prisoner at the Dnieper in July, 1709, and conveyed to Moscow and Kazan. He had fought at Narva, Clissow, Frauenstadt and Poltava. He was released, became Field-Marshal, and died in 1748.

arts, which were almost unknown before their arrival.' Bell again went to Persia, and then was on a mission, in 1737, to Constantinople. He married, in 1746, a Russian subject, Marie Peters; left the Russian service; had a career as a Turkey merchant; and, finally, died at Antermony, aged 89, on 1st July, 1780.

Another Scot, a more humble adherent of the Great Tsar, was one of those 500 Scots and English whom he picked up during his residence in England. He was 'Mr. Farquharson[1] (an able mathematician), a Scots Highlander,' whom he took with him from England to Holland and Russia, and who taught Moscow youths arithmetic in a room in the Souchareva Bashnya before he was transported to St. Petersburg. Major-General Chambers was made a Knight of St. Andrew after the taking of Narva. Alexander Magnus Anderson, Major of the Österbotten regiment, went over from the Swedes to the Russians in 1712, but was later sent to Siberia with many other Scoto-

[1] Most likely the Professor Farquharson (wrongly spelled) of St. Petersburg mentioned in Dr. Cook's book.

Swedes, whose descendants have become Russians. Duncan Robertson, son of Alexander Robertson, 12th Laird of Strowan, was 'highly esteemed' by the Tsar, rose to the rank of Colonel, and died in Sweden in 1718, leaving a daughter by his wife—a Robertson of Inches.[1] Gordons come galore. Count James Gordon was wounded 'in the ancle' at Notteburg, near Narva. James Patrickovitch Gordon, as we have seen, was captured at Narva, escaped and rose to be a Brigadier. Another James Gordon we hear of being taken prisoner in 1704 and suffering 'misirabill bondeg' with the Swedes. But a far greater man than any of these, one who made his mark upon the country of his adoption, was Admiral Thomas Gordon, whom we have already mentioned. He had left the British Navy on account of his Jacobite proclivities and was found by Peter in Holland. Peter snapped him up, and he entered the Russian Navy (another Scot was in it, one William Hay, dismissed in 1724) in 1717 as Captain Commander. In 1719 he was Rear-

[1] Douglas's *Baronage of Scotland*, p. 409.

Admiral. In 1721 he commanded the squadron of Kronstadt, consisting of six battleships, three frigates and two smaller vessels. He had several *fracas* with the Dane, Rear-Admiral Sievers, but they were 'reconciled' officially. He knew no Russian, but talked to Prince Menschikoff (and this again shows the receptive powers of this favourite of the Great Tsar) in fluent Dutch. He captured Danzig in 1724; was Commander-in-Chief at Kronstadt in 1727; resigned and was re-appointed in 1733, and held the appointment until his death. Kronstadt owes everything to him and to his master, except what it owes to Admiral Greig in later times.

He died at his post, at Kronstadt (during the regency of Anna Leopoldovna), 18th March, 1741, when the Jacobites, who had made much of him, announced that the Chevalier de St. George regretted 'the honnest Admiral very much.' The Admiral married Margaret Ross, the widow of William Monypenny (of the Pitmilly family). She died before 9th January, 1721-2, and was buried near the grave of the

1719 he piloted the Russian fleet into Nörrköping, stole the bones of St. Henry (English) from the Cathedral of Åbo, carrying them off to St. Petersburg. Hence the very name of Otto was held in horror among the Finns. The more wicked he became the more honours were lavished upon him, till, when on a commission in Livonia, he caused a noble of high rank to be whipped to death. This was more than even the Czar could stand. Count Otto was advised to retire to his vast estates, where he was still living in 1763, at that time seventy-six years of age.' To this charming biography Dr. Otto Donner[1] adds that he was a son of Count Gustaf Douglas and grandson of General Count Robert Douglas (of the Whittinghame family), the first of the name in Sweden. Both he and his brother Wilhelm were taken prisoners at Poltava and conveyed to Vologda. There he entered the Russian service at the age of thirty. He was made Governor-General of Finland in 1717. Dr. Donner continues: 'violent in temper,

[1] *A Brief Sketch of the Scottish Families in Finland and Sweden*, by Otto Donner (Helsingfors, 1884).

Arsenius, Metropolitan of Thebais, who was then in England, and with the Patriarchs of Constantinople, Alexandria, Jerusalem, Antioch, Heraclea, Nicomedia, Chalcedon, and Thessalonica, with powers to treat with all the Orthodox Greek or Russian Churches. On the Tsar's death the project died also, but it is worthy of much study, especially as, romantic though it seemed then, it was the precursor of the *rapprochement* between the Orthodox and the Anglican Churches in the nineteenth and twentieth centuries.

But the most romantic thing, and a thing of horror in Peter the Great's reign, is unquestionably the execution of Mary Danielovna Hamilton in 1719. Mary Hamilton was of that family that gave his mother her tincture of Western freedom and culture, and was introduced to his dangerous Court to wait on the Empress Catherine, the Livonian ex-peasant. The Tsar, *on dit*, fell in love with her. But she favoured others, and one especially, it is said, an Orloff. Children were born of her guilty connection, and she destroyed them. Russian

contents of the Academy of St. Petersburg, a description which only an ex-medical student could have written.

'Here I saw the head of the unfortunate Miss Hamilton, a Swedish lady,[1] who lost it for having murdered her child, unlawfully begotten; and this is the only murder of that kind I ever heard of in Russia. This lady was maid of honour to the Empress Catherine. It is said Peter went and saw her executed. He wept much, but could not prevail with himself to pardon her, for fear, as is said, that God would charge him with the innocent blood she had shed. He caused her head to be cupped, and injected. The forehead is almost compleat; the face is the beautifullest my eyes ever beheld; the *dura mater* and brain are all preserved in their natural situation. This is kept in spirits, in a large chrystal vessal.'

[1] This is what makes me think the Hamiltons came to Russia *viâ* Sweden.

VII.

We learn a good deal about the doings of the Bruce family in Russia from the memoirs of Peter Henry Bruce,[1] who served in the Prussian, Russian, and British armies successively. He narrates that two Bruces, James and John, cousins, both of the family of Airth, agreed during 'the troubles of Oliver Cromwell,' to push their fortunes abroad. They desired to go together, but got by mischance into two ships at Leith, one of which went to Russia and one to Prussia, and so never met again! James Bruce was the founder of the Russian branch, but it is from the grandson of the Prussian John that we learn most about their

[1] *Memoirs of Peter Henry Bruce, Esq., a military officer in the services of Prussia, Russia, and Great Britain*, printed for the author's widow, London, 1782.

doings. Peter Henry Bruce (John's grandson, born in 1692) was in the Prussian army, and saw much soldiering in the Netherlands during the Blenheim campaign. It was not until 1710 that he entered the Russian service by the invitation (it is a wonderful instance of clannish feeling) of General James Bruce, who was son of Colonel William Bruce and grandson of the James Bruce who had been carried to Russia and was now one of the right-hand men of Peter the Great, and head of the Ordnance at Moscow. He joined his cousin at Warsaw on the 17th May, he being there in attendance on the Tsar, and at Taweroff, on the 29th, the Tsar was privately married to Catherine Alek-sievna (the Livonian ex-peasant), and on this occasion General Bruce, who was present, was made Master-General of the Ordnance. He was already knight of four Orders, St. Andrew, the White Eagle, the Black Eagle and the Elephant. The campaign of the Pruth followed, Prince [illegible] letter being read at the council of war which the Tsar called in General Bruce's tent. When peace was made Peter

went off on one of those curious tours to Germany, taking General Bruce with him, while the latter's young relative was sent on an embassy to Constantinople, not returning from thence to Peterhof until 13th October. Peters-burg was then in its infancy and houses scarce, and it is interesting to find that young Bruce had another protector there of his kin. 'I had the good fortune to be accomodated in Lieutenant-General (Roman Vilemovitch) Bruce's house, who was commandant of Peters-burg,[1] and brother to the Master-General of the Ordnance,' but the last, being still in Germany, ordered him to occupy his own house in Moscow, 'and stay in his house with his lady till he should arrive.' In this way we get the following description of Moscow in 1713: 'Coming in view of it, in a clear sunshine day,

[1] His career was this: born 1668, he probably accompanied the Tsar Peter on his travels, 1697-98. He took part in the Siege of Schlüsselburg. In [illegible] he was made commandant of St. [illegible], and till his death, in 1720, was occupied in building the town. He was buried in the Fort of St. Peter and St. Paul (which he built) beside the Cathedral, opposite the altar. It was through his influence that the first Evangelical Church, St. Anne's, was built in St. Petersburg.

I never saw so glorious a sight as this city presented at a distance, with the vast numbers of gilded domes and steeples; but my expectations were greatly disappointed when I entered it, finding only ill-built wooden houses, and timber-streets interspersed with churches, and brick-houses with large courts and gardens, the habitations of the grandees and people of fortune; and coming to General Bruce's house, I met with a very kind reception from his lady, who treated me with the affection of a mother: they had then no child.'

He was witness of the 'great and dreadful fire' which broke out 'in a maiden monastery outside the town,'[1] which 'consumed the greatest part of the city, especially the wooden houses,' and was astonished to see how soon it was rebuilt. Moscow was in a transition

[1] Probably the Novo Devichi monastery. Founded in 1524, it was to it that the Tsaritza Irina, sister of Boris Godounoff, retired, and in it Maria, widow of Magnus, King of Livonia, niece of Ivan the Terrible, was 'shut up' by Boris Godounoff (the editor of Horsey's *Travels* (Hakluyt Society) confuses it with the Troitza, where she was ultimately buried). Later, the Tsarevna Sophia, Regent, who was forced to become the Nun Susanna, as we have seen, by her brother Peter the Great, was interned here.

the Tsarevitch, Aleksei Petrovitch, whom he thought meanly of. The Tsar absolutely disregarded his subjects' discomfort in the new capital,[1] being wholly intent upon its progress and that of Kronstadt. 'It was surprising to see so many great things undertaken and put in execution by one single person, without the assistance and help of anyone; his own great genius and indefatigable application to things, presiding over all, and seeing everything with his own eyes ... so that never monarch was less imposed on than himself.' Petersburg had to be glazed with glass from England, but the Tsar erected large manufactories for making window and looking glass, under the direction of Englishmen, at Moscow. In 1716 young Bruce was commanded to discipline thirty tall

[1] It was his own creation. 'He found only four fishermen's huts, to which he added a house for himself on an island for himself, on an island in the north side of the river, and called it Petersburg. This house was only a shelter from the weather and to rest in ... but in memory of this great undertaking, it has been preserved ever since. Lieutenant-General Robert Bruce, commandant of the city, has the charge and use of this original hall, and has built a very good house adjoining to it for himself, which was one of the first that made a show in this place.'

advantage of each particular work, to which he gave his answers so readily . . . that his grandfather was so well pleased, that he embraced him most heartily, and made him a present of his picture richly set with diamonds, and gave him an ensign's commission in the first regiment of guards.' In 1721 Peter Bruce heard he had succeeded to a small estate in Scotland, and begged Count Bruce to get him leave to go thither, but the inexorable Tsar refused, until his own pleasure. The triumphal entry to Moscow was in the air. This triumphal entry was followed by 'six weeks' feasting,' and then on 22nd February, 1722, a proclamation was made 'by the sound of trumpet,' to acknowledge the successor to the throne, whom the autocrat should nominate. 'The order, however, must be obeyed, and was complied with by many with a reluctant heart . . . this was to me the most disagreeable service I ever performed in Russia, as I was so well acquainted with the excellent temper and genius of the young prince (Peter Aleksievitch), having had the honour to teach him the military exercises and fortification, and to whose prejudice this oath was certainly administered.'

The Caspian and Persian campaigns and many détours in Russia followed before the Scot obtained his 'liberty.' In 1724 things went a little better, and he was told that 'as soon as the Empress Catherine's coronation was over' he would receive his dispatches. Moscow hummed with foreigners and natives for this event, and at the ceremony he recounts that 'No. 13, Count Bruce, a privy counsellor and master of the horse,' carried the crown, his wife, 'the Countess of Bruce,' following as one of the train-bearers of the Empress herself. Peter Bruce was offered more preferment, and did not get his furlough from Count Bruce's representation to Prince Menschikoff until 27th May, 1724. Even then he 'received the pay and forage money due to me from the regiment, but could not get the two years' pay that was due to me as Engineer, and which amounted to twelve hundred rubles, but was told the money appropriated for the payment of the service was at Petersburg, and I must go there to receive it, which, if I had done, would have effectually put a stop to my journey. I empowered Major-General Le Fort to receive my pay, and sell my house and furniture in Petersburg, and to remit me the money to Scotland, but a stop was put to it till my return, and at the expiration of my furlough, everything I had left there was seized, so that I had no reason to boast of any advantage I reaped in Russia after thirteen years' service.'[1]

In those times it was much easier getting into Russia than out of it, as was evident in the case of Major-General Gordon, who 'wanted very much to quit the service, and solicited his discharge by every application in his power, but all in vain; and, being in Poland on a separate command,' after the battle of Poltava, 'he took that opportunity to send to Moscow for his wife and daughters, and on their arrival in Poland he carried them to Danzig, where he took shipping and sailed for Scotland.'[2]

[1] He went into the British service, and in 1745 helped to fortify Berwick. He retired soon afterwards, and died in 1757.

[2] *Memoirs of Peter Henry Bruce*, p. 114.

VIII.

THE short and tumultuous reign of Peter's widow, the Tsaritza Catherine I., did nothing to attract foreigners. Short though it was, that of his grandson her successor, Peter II., brought at least one Scot of great distinction to Russia, in the person of General James Francis Edward Keith, now perhaps best known as the inventor of *Kriegspiel.* Born in Scotland in 1696, the younger son of the Earl Marischal of Scotland and Lady Mary Drummond, James Keith, 'having an elder brother (the last Earl Marischal, the friend of Frederick the Great), was intitled to no other designation but simply that of his name, as the family honours, in many estates of Europe, belong exclusively to the eldest son'[1] Of a fervent Jacobite stock,

[1] *A Discourse on the Death of Marshal Keith*, kindly lent me by W. Keith Murray, Esq.

both he and his brother were 'out' in the '15 and, being attainted, lost their all and were forced to take service under other flags. At first he entered that of Spain, but, being a Protestant, advancement was impossible, so he fixed his eyes on Russia, and with a brevet of Major-General from the Emperor, arrived there in 1729, and 'immediately gained the good graces of the young sovereign, Peter II. (partly taught in military matters by the Scot, Captain Bruce, as we have seen), and who gave him a Lieutenant-Colonel's commission in a new regiment of guards, which was just levied, and of which Count Lowenwolde was Colonel. He rose rapidly, 'because he always did his duty as a brave officer, without intermeddling with any State intrigues'—and there were the Dolgoroukis, one of whom, Princess Catherine Aleksievna Dolgoroukaya,[1] became the Tsar's *fiancée*, against the Menschikoffs during the

[1] Keith had a poor opinion of her brother, Prince Ivan, the Tsar's mentor, and pronounced him to be 'one much fitter to direct a pack of hounds (which had been his study the greatest part of his life), than such a vast empire.'—*Memoirs of Marshal Keith*, pp. 80-81.

Tsar's short reign—till Peter II. died in 1730. Keith at once took the oath to the new Empress, Anna Ivanovna, Duchess of Courland (Peter the Great's niece), who was brought out of her obscurity at Mittau to please the oligarchic party, and was made Lieutenant-Colonel of her bodyguard, 'an emploiement looked on as one of the greatest trusts in the empire.' When the Polish war came on in 1733, he found himself serving under the Irish Catholic, General de Lacy. After the fall of Danzig in 1734, he was made Lieutenant-General. However successful, Keith did not like the task of coercing Poland, deeming the duty 'not a very honourable one.' His next service was the German war, and then against the Turks in the Ukraine. In this, successful though it was, Keith protested against the Russo-German General Münnich's waste of human life, and being wounded in the knee at Otchakoff, 2nd July, 1737, was incapacitated for the rest of the campaign. 'I had sooner,' said the Empress Anna, 'lose ten thousand of my best soldiers than Keith.' He was able, therefore, to visit

Paris and London, where he was now viewed, not as a Jacobite exile, but as a great General. He returned to Russia and was made Governor of the Ukraine, and his humane rule made him considered one of the best Governors the unfortunate Ukraine had ever had.

On the death of[1] the Empress Anna Ivanovna, 28th October, 1740, her grandnephew, Ivan Antonovitch (of Brunswick) was declared Emperor. For twenty-two days her favourite, Johann Ernst Biron, Duke of Courland, acted as Regent, and then, by a palace revolution, the boy Tsar's mother, Anna Leopoldovna, was declared Regent. Her rule was weak, and ended suddenly on 25th November, 1741, when her mother's cousin, Elizabeth, the younger daughter of Peter the Great, threw off her usual lassitude, put herself at the head of her Guards, assumed the title of Empress, and sent the deposed royal family packing to Kholmogory, in strict custody and into lifelong exile. We are told that 'Mr. Keith acknowledged the new Sovereign with-

[1] Alexander Gordon, a son of John Gordon, of Glenbucket, in the Russian Navy, was killed in 1740 fighting against the Turks.

out hesitation; and after the example of his friend and countryman, Lascy (Lacy), took the oath of allegiance' again. Before her accession he fought against Sweden, and aided in the reduction of Willmannstrand.[1] The Swedish campaign continued during Elizabeth's reign, and did not finish until the capture of Helsingfors and the Åland Islands forced the cession of Karelia to Russia. Service under Elizabeth was less agreeable to foreigners than that under Anna, and we find that Generals Keith, Lowendahl, Lieven, Douglas, all wished to retire. Keith was, to pacify him, offered the command in chief against the Persians and the Order of St. Andrew, but he only accepted the last. War with Sweden broke out again, and he was employed, always with success; and he was later both Commander-in-Chief of the Russian forces and Minister-plenipotentiary to Sweden, receiving swords of honour galore. He was in the Prussian campaign in 1745, and next year had his troops reviewed by the Empress at Narva.

[1] It was here that he met an orphan prisoner, Eva Merthens, whom he educated. To her and her children by him he left all his money.

His position was, however, not comfortable, and his commands were removed one by one. It is said that the amorous Empress wished to marry him, and he feared Siberia if he refused. Be that as it may, he did not like the Russian service; his brother was forbidden, as a Jacobite, to visit him at Riga, and he eventually obtained his dismission and slipped away, to die gloriously as Marshal Keith at the battle of Hochkirchen, 14th October, 1758,[1] in the service of Frederick the Great. We are told that he spoke six languages, and had 'seen all the Courts of Europe, great and small, from that of Avignon to the residence of the Khan of Tartary, and accommodated himself to every place as if it had been his native country. General, minister, courtier, philosopher—all these characters, however different in themselves, were in him united.' Certainly a great

[1] A much fuller account of his career is given in Hill Burton's *Scot Abroad*. Some interesting letters showing his difficulties in the Russian service are given in the Report of Lord Elphin-[illegible] (*Historical MSS. Commission, IXth Report*). A letter of his, written from the camp of Fascula, 1st Sept., 1741, mentions 'the Scots merchants who are settled at Petersburg receiving letters from Edinburgh every week.'

man. With Marshal Keith in Russia was a cousin, Sir Robert Keith, 5th Bart. of Ludquhairn. He served there fifteen years, and was in most of the campaigns in Poland, Germany, Turkey and Sweden. After the General's death, he entered the Danish service. He married Margaret Albertina Conradina von Suchin, daughter of the Saxon envoy to Russia, and left a family.[1]

Another of Elizabeth's Scottish Generals was General John Fullarton, of Dudwick. He remained (with General Brown, styled 'an Englishman') in the Empress's service after most of the other foreign officers. He died, surrounded by Russian servants, unmarried, in Scotland, at the end of the eighteenth century.

We get an account of part of the reigns of Anna Ivanovna and Elizaveta Petrovna in the writings of Dr. John Cook,[2] who went to Russia in 1735. He mentions many Scottish doctors

[1] Douglas's *Baronage of Scotland*, p. 75.

[2] *Voyages and Travels through the Russian Empire, Tartary, and part of the Kingdom of Persia*, by John Cook, M.D. at Hamilton; Edinburgh, 1768.

in St. Petersburg—Lewis Calderwood, who went to Russia in 1728, as surgeon to the Preobrajenski Guards, and was employed in Moscow and St. Petersburg hospitals until he died, in 1755—and Dr. James Mounsey (from Lochmaben), who was afterwards made Physician to the Empress Elizabeth, and who later introduced rhubarb as a medicine into Great Britain; Mr. Selkirk, 'surgeon to the Guards,' and Mr. Malloch. Scots bristle through his volumes, from great 'Russian merchants'[1] like Mungo Graeme, of Garvock, down to 'Peter Miln, who had been nine years keeping the books for "Mr. Demidoff" belonging to his great ironworks in Siberia.' In the wars with Turkey, in 1736-1739, he resided in 'Taverhoff,' and gives a pretty good account of the military

[1] Allan Ramsay wrote a poem to Mr. Donald MacEwan, 'Jeweller at St. Petersburg,' which has the verses:

> It is the mind that's not confin'd
> To passions mean and vile,
> That's never pin'd, while thoughts refin'd
> Can gloomy cares beguile.
>
> Then Donald may be e'en as gay
> On Russia's distant shore,
> As on the Tay, where usquebae
> He us'd to drink before.

operations. He mentions, in 1737, General Leslie, 'a gentleman of Scots extraction,' who with his troops refused to surrender to the Tartars, and died like men. A Mr. Innes, lieutenant in the Horse Guards, from Aberdeen, was a volunteer under Münnich, and helped to stop some cruelties. He rose, by bravery, to the rank of a Colonel of Dragoons during the war, but was killed before its end. He calls him 'The brave Innes, the soldiers' friend, and beloved of all good men.' A Colonel Johnston—'old Johnston,' Cook familiarly names him—'a Scotsman from Kenneil,' flits across his pages; and one Lieutenant Glassford, Commandant of the port of Earkee, is several times mentioned. Most interesting of all is his description of the Empress Elizabeth herself, whom the deluded Jacobites so fondly hoped Prince Charlie would marry. 'She was of a large stature, and inclineable to be fat, but extremely beautiful; and in her countenance I saw so much mildness and majesty, that I cannot in words express them. Her hair was black, and her skin white as "snow unsunn'd." . . . At this time Count Razumovski (Aleksei Gregorievitch Razumovski) was attending her Majesty. It is really surprising that a fat, though young woman, could move so cleverly as the Empress did, in so much that I could scarce hear her feet upon the floor; but indeed her august presence had much disconcerted me.'[1]

[1] *Voyages and Travels through the Russian Empire, Tartary, and part of the Kingdom of Persia*, by John Cook, M.D. at Hamilton, ii. p. 570; Edinburgh, 1768.

CHAPTER

SCOTTISH FAMILIES SETTLED
COURT PHYSICIANS. RO
SCOTS—SIR JAMES WYLIE,
DE TOLLY, LERMONTOFF.

IX.

Peter III., the nephew and heir of the Empress Elizabeth, had but a short reign, being, after reigning a few months, deposed by his wife, Sophia of Anhalt-Zerbst, who, after his murder, ruled as Catherine II., or as Catherine the Great, from 1762 to 1796. Taking up the mantle of Peter the Great, she made the Russian people her own by becoming one of themselves. It was not so much that she did not encourage foreigners as well, for she did, but all her chief favourites were Russians, and it was to them that she gave the chief power, and to everything she carefully gave a Russian dress. Times, also, had changed. Russia was no longer the backward Byzantine empire it had been when Peter I. began to reign. He had battered down the wall that had separated it from Western Europe, and by the time Catherine came to occupy his throne, a class of Westernised Russians with Western ideas—mainly French, but in part German—had grown up. The use of the Scots naturally became much less, but there were still several names of note. The Bruces, now a Russified family, were powerful at Court. Count James Alexandrovitch Bruce, born 1742, fought against the Swedes, and was Governor of Moscow in 1781-86. He died at St. Petersburg in 1790-91, being buried in the Monastery of St. Alexander Nevski.[1]

Another Count Bruce (uncle?) was Senator, Lieutenant-General of the Semenovski Guards, General-in-Chief, and Governor of Novgorod and Tver. His wife was Prascovia Alexandrovna Roumiantsova, sister of the great General Roumiantsoff.[2] She was born 7th October, [illegible], and married in [illegible]. She was one

[1] He had one daughter, who married into the family of Mysin-Pushkin, and took the name of Bruce, but had no children.

[2] K. Waliszewski, *Story of a Throne*, p. 380.

as much as in medicine, and it is through his hands that the bribes are supposed to pass, I cannot but be very pleased at his absence.'[1] Anyway, he was honoured by the complete confidence of his Imperial mistress, and retained that of her son, the Emperor Paul.

Clarke[2] gives a delightful anecdote of him. 'Dr. Rogerson,' he says, 'as we were informed, regularly received' (from his patients' hands) 'his snuff-box, and as regularly carried it to a jeweller for sale. The jeweller sold it again to the first nobleman who wanted a fee for his physician; so that the doctor obtained his box again, and at last the matter became so well understood between the jeweller and the physician, that it was considered by both parties as a sort of banknote, and no words were necessary in transacting the sale of it.' These 'bank notes' allowed Dr. Rogerson to acquire the lands of Wamphray, in his native Dumfriesshire, and to maintain some state, and to build the house of Dumcrieff, where he died in

[1] K. Waliszewski, *The Story of a Throne*, p. 389.
[2] *Travels*, pp. 113-4.

1823. The grateful Empress presented him with a collection of casts of all the medals struck by her Grand Ducal or Imperial predecessors (the 'False Dimitri' is, oddly enough, omitted, *pour cause*?), which, in a delightful eighteenth century case still exist.[1]

Though Dr. Rogerson, Dr. Guthrie and Sir James Wylie (of whom we shall hear later) were the chief physicians in the reigns of Catherine and Paul, and political powers, we are told that: 'Persons calling themselves *English Physicians* are found in almost every town' in Russia. 'Sometimes they have served in apothecaries' shops in *London* and *Edinburgh*; but generally they are Scots apothecaries who are men of Professional Skill and acknowledged Superiority.[2] At St. Petersburg the Court Banker, Sutherland, was a Scot. Catherine made Robert Rutherford (fourth son of Sir John Rutherford of that ilk, who died unmarried), for many years a merchant in Leghorn, a

[1] The author's grandfather acquired them from Dr. Rogerson's son, and they are now in the author's possession. He reproduces three as illustrations to this book.
[2] Clarke's *Travels*, p. 114.

Baron of the Russian Empire; and one of the Court Painters (who accompanied the Tsaritsa in her celebrated Progress to Crimea with Potemkin) bore the Scottish name of John Lindsay.

It was the maritime needs of the Russian Empire that brought the true worth of the Scots to the great mind of the Empress Catherine. She recruited many Scots from the British Navy, the chief of whom were Admirals Greig and Elphinstone. The Scots made a great name in the land of their adoption, and the Russian Navy owes everything to them. Samuel Carlovitch Greig, of Inverkeithing in Fife, went to Russia in 1763, with five other British officers, mostly Scots. He destroyed the Turkish fleet in 1770,[1] with his fire-ships, showing, with Lieutenant Drysdale, extraordinary heroism, and was hailed, from

[1] The doings of Greig and Elphinstone [illegible] will be [illegible] *Narrative of the Russian Expedition against the Turks by Sea and Land*; London, 1772. Other Scots mentioned are Mackenzie and Glasgow. Also the Englishman, Dugdale, who became an Admiral. An account of Greig is also in the *Dictionary of National Biography*.

kindly, and that the *enlèvement* was wholly characteristic of the time.

The Greig family settled in Russia. The Admiral was friendly to his compatriots. Robert Simpson, one of his Fleet Surgeons in 1774, became in 1792 Chief Surgeon of the great Naval hospital of Kronstadt. The Admiral's son, Sir Alexis Greig, entered the Russian Navy, and for remonstrating with the Emperor Paul for the latter's severity to some British seamen, was exiled in 1801 for a short time to Siberia, but he became an Admiral, and commanded in 1828 at the siege of Varna. His son, Vorontzoff Greig, later fought on the Russian side in the Crimean War, and was killed at Inkermann.

John Elphinstone, the other Scottish Admiral, whose kinsman had been in Ivan Groznie's army, died in 1785, but in England. He had begun by being *le desiré* of the Empress, but his opposition to her favourite of the time, Alexis Orloff, soon weakened his popularity. In fact he as Admiral had been the real hero of the battle of Tchesmé, but the Empress

was anxious to praise a Russian to give popularity to her alien-born rule, and gave all the laurels to Orloff. One branch of the Elphinstones remained in the Russian service. The Admiral's eldest son, Samuel William, became a Captain in the Navy, and married the daughter of his father's colleague, Admiral Kruse. His descendants are enrolled among the nobles of Livonia. John Carr gives an anecdote of an Elphinstone of the third generation in St. Petersburg at Kameni Ostrov [1]

'After the battle between the Russian and Swedish fleets off Cronstadt in May, 1790, Captain Elphinstone, then a very young lieutenant, was dispatched by his uncle, Admiral Creuse, to Catherine, who was at that time at the palace of Tsarko Selo, with the account of the successful manœuvres of her fleet . . . Young Elphinstone arrived at the palace late at night in his fighting clothes, covered with dust and gunpowder, and severely fatigued with long and arduous duty. His dispatches were instantly

[1] *Travels Around the Baltic*, by John Carr (1804); London, 1805, pp. 355-7.

carried to the Empress, who ordered her page-in-waiting to give the bearer refreshments and a bed, and requested that he might on no account be disturbed.' Catherine sent three times, but still he slept. 'At length Captain Elphinstone in all his *dishabille*' (*sic*, the author was a Scot and probably talked of '*dishabillies*') 'was conducted to her presence by her Secretary, when she commenced an enchanting conversation, in which she complimented the gallantry and many naval achievements of his family; . . . calling him "My son," "Now let proceed to business; I have received the dispatches, which have afforded me infinite satisfaction; I thank you for your bravery and zeal; I beg you will describe to me the position of the ships."' Captain Elphinstone did so, and she took a note upon her pocket-book. Then 'as she gave her orders to the Commander-in-Chief, she presented him with a rouleau of ducats, a beautiful little French watch, and, although very young, promoted him to the rank of Captain.'

The services of these Scotsmen were in-

Elphinstone, daughter of Lord Elphinstone). He had been manager of the Carron Iron Company, which had become embarrassed. Then, luckily for himself, he received, through the medium and influence of Admiral Greig, an offer from the Empress to cast shells, guns and shot for her army. Taking his workmen with him, he stole off from Scotland and went to Russia, where he formed a factory at Petrozovodsk, near Lake Onega, and also managed the mines of Olonetz. He flourished there (as did his successor Wilson, who was given the rank of General, and Charles Baird, who manufactured guns at Kronstadt and became a Knight of St. Vladimir, who both went out with him); was made a Councillor and a Knight of St. Vladimir; and died, leaving a large fortune, at St. Petersburg, 1st August, 1806. He had three daughters by his first wife, who were Anne, Countess of Haddington; Elizabeth, wife of George Augustus Pollen, Esquire, M.P., drowned at Memel in 1808; and another, who married Baron Polterazki, and died at Petrozovodsk, 11th December, 1795.

'apoplexy,' which gave the Court great satisfaction, and he remained in the highest favour. He founded the Medico-Chirurgical Academy of St. Petersburg (it has his statue), and died full of honours in 1854, leaving his money to the Tsar, who endowed with it the hospital he had built.

The other Scot who has a statue in St. Petersburg belongs really to the reign of Alexander I., the last Emperor who comes within the scope of this book, Prince Barclay de Tolly. The story of the family is this. They came to Russia during the times of the Revolution of 1688, from Towy (Tolly) in Aberdeenshire. A descendant became Burgomaster of Riga, and his son, Gottleib Barclay de Tolly, was ennobled—as a Russian officer, taking the name 'Bogdan'—and married a Mlle. Wermelen.

His sons were: (1) Bogdan Bogdanovitch (formerly Emil Johann), a General in the Russian service; (2) Michael Bogdanovitch, of whom afterwards; and (3) Andrei Bogdanovitch, a Colonel. Michael Bogdanovitch, whose statue adorns the Nevski Prospekt, opposite to the

Weimarn was allowed to take the title of Barclay de Tolly-Weimarn.

The Comte de Balmain, of the Scottish family of Ramsay of Balmain, was in the same reign the Russian Commissioner appointed to watch Napoleon, after his fall, at Saint Helena. He married, when there, the step-daughter of Sir Hudson Lowe, Miss Johnson. Lord Rosebery[1] tells us that his family had been settled in Russia for a century and a quarter.

Another Russo-Scot who fought against Napoleon was Alexander Amatus Thesleff (of a Viborg family), born in 1788, a Lieutenant-Colonel in 1812. He was Assistant Governor-General of his native Finland from 1832 to 1847.

A Russian of Scottish descent, born in 1813, glorified his country in the reign of Alexander I. This was the great romantic poet Michael Yourievitch Lermontoff. His grandfather was Peter Lermontoff, whose ancestors, of the same blood as that which produced, ages before, the

[1] *Napoleon, the Last Phase*, p. 142.

what his parents had taught him of the value of Scottish physicians. He employed two Crichtons, uncle and nephew, of the old family of Frendraught, as his own physicians, who will be the last of the long roll of Scotsmen whom Russia has taken to itself, to be mentioned in this book. The first was Sir Alexander Crichton,[1] a son of Alexander Crichton of Newington, born at Edinburgh in 1763. He entered the Emperor's service in 1804 as Physician in Ordinary, and was soon made head of the whole civil medical department. He died, full of honours, in England, on 4th June, 1856. The second was his nephew, Sir Alexander William Crichton, born in 1791. He married, in 1820, the daughter of Dr. Sutthoff, another of the Court Physicians.

Decorated and caressed by the Russian Court, and knighted by George IV. in 1817, he was made a member of the Medical Council and a Councillor of State. He was thirty years

[1] An account is given in the *Dictionary of National Biography*, and a short one of his nephew as well in Anderson's *Scottish Nation*, vol. i. pp. 726, 727.

INDEX

INDEX

CPSIA information can be obtained
at www.ICGtesting.com
Printed in the USA
BVOW06s1500140917
494908BV00017B/156/P

9 781333 795467